First Facts®

Water in Our World

The Water Cycle at Work

by Rebecca Olien

raintree

Raintree is an imprint of Capstone Global Library Limited, a company incorporated in England and Wales having its registered office at 264 Banbury Road, Oxford, OX2 7DY – Registered company number: 6695582
www.raintree.co.uk
myorders@raintree.co.uk

Text © Capstone Global Library Limited 2016

ISBN 978-1-4747-1221-7
19 18 17 16 15
10 9 8 7 6 5 4 3 2 1

British Library Cataloguing in Publication Data
A full catalogue record for this book is available from the British Library.

Editorial Credits
Abby Colich, editor; Kyle Grenz, designer; Wanda Winch, media researcher; Laura Manthe, production specialist

Photo Credits
Capstone, 7; Corbis: Joe McBride, 11; Shutterstock: DrimaFilm, 1, Ecelop, waves design, grublee, 8, JaroPienza, 18, Julia Kurm, 13, Kotenko Oleksandr, cover, Nadalina, 5, papa studio, 14-15, paula french, 20, Radu Bercan, 16-17, tachyglossus, splash design

Every effort has been made to contact copyright holders of material reproduced in this book. Any omissions will be rectified in subsequent printings if notice is given to the publisher.

All the Internet addresses (URLs) given in this book were valid at the time of going to press. However, due to the dynamic nature of the Internet, some addresses may have changed, or sites may have changed or ceased to exist since publication. While the author and publisher regret any inconvenience this may cause readers, no responsibility for any such changes can be accepted by either the author or the publisher.

Printed and bound in China.

Contents

Water covers Earth

From space, Earth looks like a round, blue ball with swirls of white. The blue colour is water. The white is clouds. Water covers 70 per cent of Earth. It moves and changes as part of the water *cycle*.

cycle—something that happens over and over again

Fact!

Earth is sometimes called the Blue Planet.

The water cycle

Water changes as it moves through the water cycle. Water *evaporates* as it changes from a liquid into a gas, or *vapour*. Water vapour *condenses* to form clouds. *Precipitation* falls from clouds as rain or snow. The sun's heat turns liquid water back into gas. Then the water cycle begins again. Let's take a closer look at each part of this cycle.

evaporate—to change from a liquid to a gas
vapour—a substance in gas form
condense—to change from a gas into a liquid
precipitation—water that falls from the sky as rain, sleet, snow or hail

condensation

precipitation

evaporation

Evaporation

One way the water cycle can begin is with evaporation. During evaporation, the sun's heat makes water change from a liquid into vapour.

People can't see water vapour. Vapour can only be seen when it is mixed with water drops. You can see vapour as steam coming from a hot cup of tea.

Humidity

Humidity is the amount of water vapour in the air. Humidity changes with the temperature. Warm air holds more water vapour than cold air. People feel warmer on humid days because sweat does not evaporate quickly.

Fact!

Your hair is slightly longer on humid days. Humidity can make a strand of hair up to three per cent longer.

humidity—the measure of the moisture in the air

Condensation

A very humid day can lead to a lot of water condensation. Condensation takes place when water changes from vapour back into a liquid. Vapour turns into droplets as the air cools. You can see condensation as dewdrops on leaves. Condensation also forms on the outside of a glass of cold water.

Clouds

Clouds are another form of condensation. Vapour becomes water droplets around specks of dust in the sky. These droplets stick together to make clouds.

Clouds grow heavy with water as condensation takes place. Dark clouds are full of water. Rain is on the way.

Fact!

Fog is a cloud that's close to the ground.

Precipitation

Precipitation is the final part of the water cycle. Water falls from clouds as precipitation. Rain falls when clouds fill with water. Frozen water falls as snow, *sleet* or *hail*.

Precipitation *replenishes* water on Earth. Rain *seeps* into the soil to restore water to the ground. Rain and snow fall in rivers, lakes and oceans.

sleet—rain that freezes as it's falling and hits the ground as frozen pellets of ice

hail—small balls of ice that form in clouds during a thunderstorm

replenish—to make full again

seep—to flow or trickle slowly

Fact!

Freezing rain is rain
that freezes after it
hits the ground.

17

An endless cycle

Saving water helps make sure all living things have the freshwater they need. People, plants and animals share the same freshwater. Everyone must work together to save water and keep it clean.

Amazing but true!

The water people drink today is the same
water dinosaurs drank millions of years ago.
Earth's water is about 3 billion years old. The
water cycle keeps water on the planet. In the
future, people, plants and animals will also
use this same water.

Hands on: water cycle cups

Water is the only substance found in nature as a solid, liquid and gas. Try this activity to see how water changes into its different forms as part of the water cycle.

What you need

- 2 clear plastic cups
- hot tap water
- ice cube

What you do

1. Fill one plastic cup with about 2.5 centimetres (1 inch) of hot tap water.
2. Quickly place the second cup upside down on top of the first cup. Make sure that the rims of the cups line up.
3. Place an ice cube on top of the upper cup.
4. Look for the different states of water in the water cycle. Water vapour rises into the top cup. The ice cools the air, so tiny droplets form. As the drops get bigger, they fall back into the cup like rain.

Glossary

condense—to change from a gas into a liquid

cycle—something that happens over and over again

evaporate—to change from a liquid into a gas

hail—small balls of ice that form in clouds during a thunderstorm

humidity—the measure of the moisture in the air

precipitation—water that falls from the sky as rain, sleet, snow or hail

replenish—to make full again

seep—to flow or trickle slowly

sleet—rain that freezes as it's falling and hits the ground as frozen pellets of ice

vapour—a substance in gas form

Read more

Earth's Water Cycle (Earth's Cycles in Action), Diane Dakers (Crabtree Publishing, 2015)

Step-by-Step Experiments with the Water Cycle, Shirley Smith Duke (The Child's World, 2012)

Water Cycle (Science Readers), Torrey Maloof (Teacher Created Materials, 2015)

Websites

Water facts
http://www.sciencekids.co.nz/sciencefacts/water.html

The water family water conservation game
http://www.thewaterfamily.co.uk/

The Water Education Foundation water facts for kids
http://www.watereducation.org/water-kids

Comprehension questions

1. Name and describe one part of the water cycle.
2. Reread pages 12 and 14 and study the photos. How are the two forms of condensation alike? How are they different?
3. Page 16 says that precipitation replenishes water to the Earth. Why is this a necessary part of the water cycle?

Index